Dear Lauren, Love Mom

31 DAYS of AFFIRMATIONS for MY DAUGHTER, for MYSELF and for YOU

D1500486

CHERYL E. WOODSON, MD
Illustrated by Brackette F. Williams, PhD

Dr. Cheryl Woodson

Straight Talk about How to Live Out Loud & Age Excellently

Dear Lauren, Love Mom: 31 Days of Affirmations for My Daughter, for Myself, and for You
Copyright ©2019 by Cheryl E. Woodson, MD • Chicago, IL

ISBN: 978-0-996-7809-2-6
Library of Congress # Pending Application Approval
November 2019

Category: Inspirational/Self-Help
Description: Inspirational affirmations to help women and their daughters

Contents

Acknowledgements

I want to thank my parents, Arthur and Beatrice Woodson, my Aunt Terri, the rest of my family, all the pastors, teachers, and inspirational authors who poured their wisdom into me, and especially, my daughter, Lauren.

Introduction

My daughter was in her early twenties when she lived through major flares of an illness she had battled in silence for several years. As a doctor, I was a strong advocate for my daughter's healthcare yet as a mother, I felt an overwhelming sense of powerlessness: I could lose my child to an adversary I couldn't even see. Lauren's care plan has taken years of painful therapies and she lives a hard-won victory that will continue to demand amazing courage. This girl has ovaries of steel. Even so, she has some very difficult days and I am proud of how she weathers her challenges.

I created some encouraging posters to reconnect Lauren to the spectacular woman she thought she had lost: the woman I foresaw when she spoke full sentences at only eighteen months, the woman I still see, the woman she is. The ideas grew out of every inspirational conversation, seminar, and book I encountered over the years. Writing has always calmed me and I was not surprised that giving voice to these feelings controlled the mom-terror and freed the doctor to fight on Lauren's behalf. However, as the words poured from my heart onto the page, I did not expect them also to seep into my spirit and heal scars from childhood hurts and adult life-stress.

In over sixty years, more than half in the practice of medicine, I have recognized hurt, little girls inside even the strongest, most capable women. This pain erodes our joy, influences our decisions, and strains our relationships. Producer, Michelle Aikens, agreed that these messages would soothe the little girls inside all of us and asked, "Why not write enough affirmations for a whole month?" My sister-in-law, Brackette Williams, offered her photographs and a book was born. Brackette also helped me choose other photos; every image harnesses the power of the Creation to complement an affirmation and make your heart and spirit soar. No matter how old you are, in these pages, you can find solace for your inner, little girl, peace to help you step out of past pain, and power to reclaim your joy.

While many of the themes reflect my specific approach to the planet, I believe each affirmation offers something to inspire women of every culture, orientation, and belief system. Pass over the ideas that don't work for you and focus on the ones most relevant to your life-experience.

Lauren gave me permission to share these thoughts with you by publishing this book. Her only stipulation was that I would not use the word "but" to join any of the phrases. She insists that this conjunction invalidates the words that come before it when all thoughts are valuable.

I welcome your feedback. Please visit www.drcherylwoodson.com to share your comments and share other resources that have encouraged and empowered you. I wish you peace. May you always look up and smile.

*I will always
remember these 5 facts...*

I am worth it

I am valuable just as I am. *I am lovable* just as I am. *I am capable* just as I am. *I am beautiful* just as I am. Although I might choose to change some things about myself, I deserve friendship, fulfillment, health, hope, joy, laughter, love, security and all good things.

Just as I am.

Resilience is key

I will understand that flexibility brings peace in the midst of the storm. *I will develop* the skills to face life's challenges and the confidence that I can take a hit and get back up. *I can learn* from the experience and come back even stronger.

> **"Blessed are the flexible for they shall not be bent out of shape."**
> ANONYMOUS*

*The author first heard it from Dr. Cynthia T. Henderson.

Control is an illusion

Even though my environment can change because of me, the changes often come from factors I cannot control (or even influence).

I will overcome behaviors that offer a fleeting semblance of control. Fake control brings only stress, guilt, and self-loathing that makes me feel even more powerless.

I will remember "The Serenity Prayer" (by Reinhold Niebuhr) and learn to accept what I cannot change. I will change what I can and seek wisdom to know the difference.

I will not expect to control everything; *I will survive* and grow, one day, one meal, one pound, one challenge, one step at a time.

Instead of chasing control, I will develop resilience.

I will not fear change

I will remember that every butterfly was once a caterpillar; both are essential stages in the life cycle.

I will understand that change is not inherently dangerous, though it can be scary, overwhelming, and even painful.

I will realize that resilience empowers me to cope with change and thrive.

Change is necessary for growth.

Courage is not the absence of fear

Courage is doing it *afraid*. When I meet an obstacle, *I will do it* and get through it!

Push that envelope, girl!

I will take care of myself

I will be kind to myself

Even as I look for ways to improve and grow...

I will give myself credit when I do well.

I will encourage myself by acknowledging and cherishing even the smallest wins.

Some people are just waiting to give me a hard time. I will stand not in line with them (at least, not in the front).

| *I will give myself the compassion I give others.* |

I will recognize that WWFU* days tell lies
*Worn and weary, fat and ugly

I will believe the *truth*. I am *not* worthless. I am *not* ugly. I am *not* stupid. The situation is *not* hopeless. I *am* lovable. Circumstances *will* improve. I *can* try again. I *can* do better next time. On WWFU days, *I will not* isolate or ruminate.

I will reach for support and *connect* with people who encourage me.
I will seek information that reinforces the truth.
I will engage in behaviors that bring positive thoughts and outcomes.

These days will pass.

It's not selfish; it's self-love

Selfish: "It's all about *me.* I do what I want, when I want, and how I want, no matter what anyone else needs."

Self-love: "It's about me, *too.* I consider my needs as well as the needs of others."

I will carve out regular time to engage in activities just because they give me joy.

I will advocate for myself, set boundaries, and insist that others respect those boundaries.

**I will not feel guilty
for loving myself.**

I will not mistake anxiety for love

I will respect myself enough to walk away from a man who is disrespectful.

I will love myself enough to walk away from a man whose behavior shows that he does not love me, even if I think he does, even if he says he does, and even if it's because he doesn't know how to love me.

I will understand that I am responsible for my own happiness. I cannot rescue, fix, or ensure happiness for someone else.

I will not pretend to be less, so a man can feel that he is more. He should be confident in his achievements and proud of mine.

I will rely on 1 Corinthians 13:4-7 (in the Bible) to learn how to recognize love.

I will compare my situation to those descriptions and walk away if the relationship falls short.

Although a man may make my life sweeter, I will remember that he does not make my life possible.

Don't hate.
Decorate!

(Sister Iris Ade, Fitness Enthusiast)

If I'm not happy with my body, *I will work* to change it. In the meantime, *I will work* with what I've got.

I will enjoy looking great, right now!

I deserve a loving relationship

I *don't need* a man to pay my bills.

I *don't need* a man who thinks I am his possession.

I *don't need* a dictator or a leech.

I *don't need* to settle for any just any kind of man.

I *shouldn't* cringe when I see his name on my caller ID.

I *deserve* a man who pays attention.

I *deserve* a man who knows I am precious.

I *deserve* a man who embraces interdependence: mutual respect, love, and support.

I *deserve* a loving life partner.

I *should* always think of him and smile.

A man may be the icing;
I am the cake.

My body belongs to me

Virginity is a state of being; chastity is a *choice*. My body is precious and worth so much more than attention, gifts, financial support, or professional advancement. My body is worth more than someone's whining and definitely, more than someone's anger. It doesn't matter what I have done in the past. The only thing that matters is what I *choose* to do, at that moment.

> ## When someone wants to touch me, it is always my choice.

I will develop a new attitude

Up is ⬆ that way

I can't look back or down and expect to move forward. *I can't change* my past. *I can learn* from it and embrace its contribution to the awesome woman I am today. *I can* and *will decide* how much power my past will have over today and my future.

| ***I will look where I want to go.*** |

Joy and happiness are not the same

When I expect to be *happy* every minute, I learn to avoid or ignore uncomfortable feelings (like anger, discouragement, fear, and sadness). Instead, *I will work* through these feelings and take away their power to erode my *joy*.

Happiness is over-the-top. It is fragile and fleeting.

Joy brings steady, deep, abiding satisfaction.

Happiness is anxious and strives for the next good feeling.

Joy rests in the knowledge that either I am on the right path or I accept myself where I am and fully commit to finding a better direction.

I will remember that happiness fades; joy endures.

Information beats panic

Whenever I begin to panic, *I will write* the answers
to these questions:

> *What do I know?*
>
> *What do I need to know?*
>
> *How can I find out?*
>
> *Who can help me?*
>
> *What am I willing to risk to make this happen?*

Clear goals and informed actions calm the chaos.

Wisdom is knowing what to do <u>next</u>

As I look over my life plan, *I will not panic* if I don't see steps A through Z. *I will finish* A, look for B, and watch C and D become clearer.

Instead of always multi-tasking or letting a huge list terrify me, *I will commit* to doing one or two things well every day.

**How can I climb a mountain?
One step at a time.**

Feelings are important

My feelings are neither good nor bad; they are mine and they are important. *I will recognize* and acknowledge my feelings. *I will not fear* them. By themselves, feelings don't affect outcome. Behavior affects outcome and *I can choose* how to behave.

I will not ignore, deny, or hide my feelings. If I do, they will only grow stronger and wrest away the power to control my behavior.

I will not allow myself to make knee-jerk responses based on my feelings. *I will feel* what I feel and take time to plan behaviors that create positive outcomes.

While *I cannot* and *should not* try to control my feelings, *I can and will decide* what to do with them.

Behavior is more important.

When life gets rough, I will...

Strive for excellence, not perfection

When I earn 97% on a test, *I will not torture* myself because I missed the other three points. *I will take* an honest look at whether I missed essential information and as I review. *I will also celebrate* what I did well. *I will refer* to that success for encouragement in the future.

I will not let "the other three points" crush my spirit.

I will always be the best me

I *will not accept* mediocrity.

I *will not bask* in the praise of people who find me impressive.

I *will listen* to my inner voice and let my spirit decide if I am where I should be.

I *will strive* for excellence, even if I am afraid, even if striving is uncomfortable.

I *will be* honest with myself about my pace and my progress.

I *will review* continually my goals and my path to be sure they are still right for me.

I *will not let* others write checks I have to cash in my health, joy, integrity, time, or future.

My best is good enough!

I will recover from "approval addiction"

(Joyce Meyer)

I will understand that some people will disagree with what I choose to do.

I will accept that some people don't have it in them to approve. They need to be negative.

I will recognize that people who truly love me want me to reach my goals. They will not try to control or manipulate me with anger, shame, or guilt; nor will they withhold love, money, or other resources.

I do not have to earn love, peace, or joy. They are my birthright.

I will understand that "rejection is just direction"

(Michele Aikens, Writer & Producer)

Even if someone doesn't want what I offer, their negative response doesn't mean that either of us is wrong. *I will find* people who fully embrace my message and serve them to the best of my ability. Even then, my resources won't always match the need. That's when *I will re-evaluate* my mission and my audience. *I will stand* ready to change what I can to be of greater service. However, *I will change* audiences rather than compromise the integrity of my message.

I will regroup, redefine, and return.

I will be fully present in this moment

Though I plan my destination, *I will savor* every step of my journey. Instead of giving in to worry about what may come (anxiety), or grief about what has passed (depression), *I will make* the best of right now. *I will do, fix, and be* what I can today.

I will own and fully experience my feelings; *I will respect* them, work through them, and not allow them to keep me from moving forward.

I will make the most of today and build a stronger foundation for my future.

I will escape from the prison of silence

I will uncover my history and let that effort release me into the abundant joy, love, peace, and success that God has promised.

I will share my story and free myself from anger, guilt, pain, and shame.

I will let others hear my story. That may free someone who has not yet found the courage to tell her story.

I will tell my story.

I will use my tools

I will forgive even "when forgiveness doesn't make sense"

(Robert Jeffress)

Forgiveness does not...

> ...mean that what happened was right or that anyone deserved it.
>
> ...demand that I maintain trust, or allow the hurt to continue.
>
> ...require that the people who hurt me are sorry or even acknowledge the hurt.

Forgiveness does...

> ...unlock the cage so I can step out, move beyond the pain of my past, and enjoy my future.
>
> ...allow me to take away people's power to hurt me any further.
>
> ...remind me also to forgive myself, learn from my mistakes, and move toward positive change.

Forgiveness frees me.

I will surround myself with people who...

Enjoy life and have a positive attitude.

Do not need me to be like them.

Always tell me the truth in love.

Respect each other's space.

Are committed to my success and their own

Share mutual support, resources, and strategies.

Give me a push when I need one.

Seek balance between career, family, friends, self and service.

Understand that jealousy questions God's power (He has more than enough for everyone); envy questions His judgment (He decides what we are and what we have); both emotions bring pain and destruction.

"Your friends are in the best position to give you a good kick in the butt, because they have your back!"
Tería Robens, Author

I will nurture a group of real friends. I will also be a real friend.

I will harness the power of "no"

I will not feel guilty when I say "No" to people and activities that distract me and siphon away my time, talents, treasures, or energy.

I will realize that I cannot want something for someone more than they want it for themselves.

I will understand that walking away from a draining situation is not giving up.

I will embrace what I heard musician/activist Nina Simone say:

"You can use up everything you've got trying to give everybody what they want."

I will learn to discern between angels and demons

When I encounter an obstacle, how can I know whether it is the enemy in my path or if God is saying, "Not this" or "Not yet"? Pastor Mike Russell from Jubilee Faith Community, Country Club Hills, IL explains it this way:

> "When God closes a door, He is refining and redirecting us. He also sends angels to encourage us, help us grow, and find the doors He has opened. It's His way of saying, 'I love you, and I will be with you always.' The enemy doesn't care about encouragement, comfort, or growth. It just wants to make the goal seem impossible."

I will remember that angels fill us with love, support, and hope, while demons leave us empty, defeated, and alone.

I will choose mentors wisely

I will consider the reputation and achievements of potential mentors and evaluate the success of their other protégés. (Have the protégés found success following their own dreams or do they only serve the mentor's agenda?) *I will also lay* the mentor's advice over my spirit, values, and goals like a template. If the advice doesn't fit, the mentors are wrong.

I will listen to my heart.

This is how I will get through each day

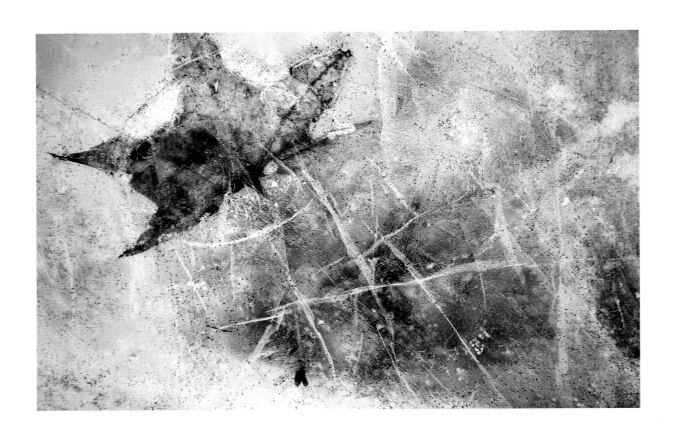

I will do "The Work" when negative thoughts try to paralyze me

From *Loving What Is* by Byron Katie (with Dr. Cheryl's explanations)

I will ask:

Is this true?

How do I know it's true? (What evidence do I have outside my own head?)

Who would I be if I didn't need this to be true? (What do I get out of believing this? How would my life be different if I didn't?)

Is there any good (me-loving, me-supporting, positive) reason to keep believing it?

**With these four questions,
I will break free and move forward.**

I will tell my inner little girl, "You can ride; you can't drive"

Just when I'm about to do something awesome, I seem to hear a little voice say, "Who do you think you are?" That's the little girl inside me. She has always heard, "No." "Girls don't do that." "You're not so special." "You're too fat." "You're not pretty enough." "You're not that smart." "Now, don't be uppity." That little girl learned to parrot what she heard. She learned to keep her dreams silent and stay invisible to protect herself from disappointment and disapproval. Her voice can erode my confidence, undermine my decisions, make me hesitate, or even avoid opportunities. When I ignore that voice and keep moving, I feel guilty about leaving my little girl behind, because it seems like I have rejected her, too.

From now on, *I will remind* myself that I do not have to leave my little girl behind and I should not. Overcoming her fears made me the capable, resourceful, compassionate woman I am today. I have grown into the woman who would have affirmed, comforted, encouraged, helped, and protected that little girl. *I will accept, love, and celebrate* my little girl. *I will hold* her hand, smile into her eyes, and tell her, "You don't have to be afraid anymore. I wasn't there when they ignored you, hurt you. Though I wasn't with you back then, I am here now and you can trust me. I've got this."

I will slide my little girl into the passenger seat and invite her to enjoy the ride as I put my hands on the steering wheel and drive my life toward joy.

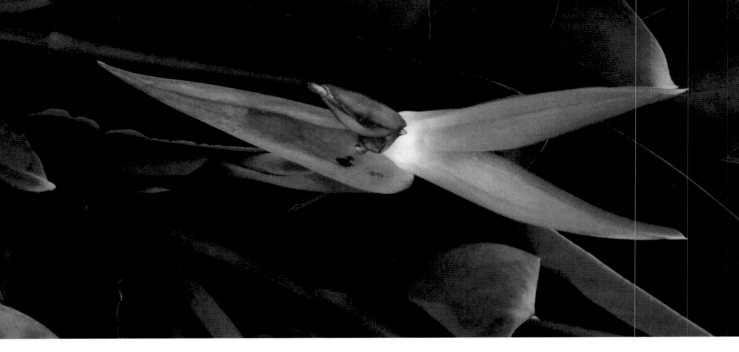

I will put myself out there

I will pretend I'm not shy. I will pretend I'm not afraid.

I will behave like I deserve to achieve my goals and eventually, my beliefs *will grow* into that behavior.

I can fake it until I feel it.

I'm also blessed with G.R.A.C.E.

I will manage money with
G.R.A.C.E.

Get professional help (a certified financial planner for budgeting, debt management, credit development, investing).

Remember to pay myself first (tithe, save, invest [20%]; live off the rest [80%]).

Avoid impulse purchases. *I will wait* at least 24 hours to see if the thing I *want* is something I *need.* That way, short-term wants *will not derail* long-term goals.

Commit to how much I'm going to spend before I shop. When the money is gone, that's it. *I will not spend more* with debit/credit cards or checks.

Eliminate lifestyle-competition. Instead of trying to match someone else's spending, *I will stick to my plan.*

> **When I manage my money, I will not have to compromise my principles, work for people I don't respect, or tolerate abusive relationships.**

I will create joy with G.R.A.C.E.

Gratitude: An attitude of gratitude generates joy!

Realism: *I can* only do what I can and will do.

Acceptance: *I will love* myself as I am right now.

Chill out! *I will* not major in the minor.

Exercise: Regular physical activity changes brain chemistry. It decreases anxiety and the perception of pain. It also increases my sense of well-being.

I will create even more joy with
G.R.A.C.E.

Great expectations: *I deserve* everything I'm willing to *work* for.

Relax: *I will seek* the destination and enjoy the journey.

Advocate for myself: *I will set* boundaries, protect them, and avoid toxic relationships and situations.

Calm down: Although *I will learn* not take everything so seriously, *I will always have* a back-up plan.

Energy: *I will generate* energy by making a commitment to my health and fitness. *I will conserve* energy by picking my battles and focusing on my goals. *I will renew* energy by getting enough rest and spending time with people and activities that I enjoy.

Meet the Contributors

In addition to "mom-ing," CHERYL E. WOODSON, MD spent more than thirty years teaching and practicing geriatric medicine. She "retired" in 2012 to focus on writing and speaking to empower families that advocate for seniors and encourage women (especially over the age of 50) to *LIVE OUT LOUD and AGE EXCELLENTLY.* She also consults with health care professionals on policies that promote wellness and avoid unnecessary hospital admissions.

Dr. Cheryl is the author of *To Survive Caregiving: A Daughter's Experience, A Doctor's Advice* and *The Doctor Is In: Answering Your Questions about How to Survive Caregiving.* She also writes romantic novels under the pseudonym, Tería Robens (TR). These books follow her characters' transition from doormat to diva and remind women that it is not too late to live their dreams. Follow Dr. Cheryl and TR on Facebook, at www.drcherylwoodson.com, blog *Straight Talk with Dr. Cheryl,* www.teríarobens.com, and blog *Juggling and Trying to Drop only the RUBBER Balls.*

BRACKETTE F. WILLIAMS, PhD is a tenured faculty member in the School of Anthropology at the University of Arizona-Tucson and a 1997 recipient of the John D. and Catherine T. MacArthur Foundation Fellowship. She has conducted ground-breaking research and published academic books and articles on nationalist ideology and identity politics in the Caribbean, as well as ethnographic studies of the death penalty and prison classification systems. As a 2008 Soros Justice Advocacy Fellow and participant in the American Friends Service Committee's campaign to remove solitary confinement from prison practices, Dr. Williams studied the impact of long-term solitary confinement on reentry into society among persons released from the Arizona Department of Corrections. Dr. Williams writes short stories and other works of fiction, does photography just for fun, and is also Dr. Woodson's sister-in-law.

Made in the USA
Monee, IL
28 August 2021